Not Ashamed

28 Devotionals for Christian Teens

by
Ed Robinson

Beacon Hill Press of Kansas City
Kansas City, Missouri

Copyright 1992
by Beacon Hill Press of Kansas City

ISBN: 083-411-4380

Printed in the United States of America

Cover illustration by Paul Franitza

Unless otherwise indicated, all Scripture quotations are from the following copyrighted version of the Bible, permission for which is acknowledged with appreciation:

The Holy Bible, New International Version (NIV), copyright © 1973, 1978, 1984 by the International Bible Society. Used by permission of Zondervan Bible Publishers.

King James Version (KJV).

10   9   8   7   6   5   4   3   2

To
Kelly Suzanne
my daughter, my friend, my sister in Christ.
I'm not ashamed to be called your dad.
It's a title I'm proud to hold.

Preface

I have been asking myself an important question lately. In the midst of a world full of phony, imitation, and pretend spirituality, what does it mean to be genuinely Christian? In fact, I have committed my life to discovering the answer. I want to be a genuine Christian. I believe it is a worthy pursuit.

I have discovered that the gospel is at the heart of authentic Christian living. The gospel is more than a formula of words on paper. It's more than a system of ideas. The gospel is God's wonderful plan for redeeming all of creation! That plan has come to life in Jesus Christ.

When the apostle Paul declared that he was not ashamed of the gospel, he was saying something very significant. He was declaring his confidence in Jesus Christ and God's ability to redeem the world.

I invite you to join me in my pursuit of authentic Christian faith. I hope in the process that we'll discover that we, like Paul, are not ashamed of the gospel either.

—Ed

Not Ashamed

I am not ashamed of the gospel, because it is the [needed] power of God for the salvation of everyone who believes (Rom. 1:16).

Have you ever thought about the questions parents and teachers ask that don't really need an answer? Once in a while I'll call home to see if our daughters have arrived safely from school. Kim or Kelly pick up the phone and say, "Hello." I always ask, "Are you home?" What is she supposed to say, "No, you're talking with a computer-generated voice machine"? Or, how about "How many times do I have to tell you to pick up your room?" What is the right answer—5, 13, or 92? Then there's the all-time favorite, "Do you want to be put on restriction?" How do you answer that—"Yes, I've been looking forward to being grounded"?

Another unanswerable parent/teacher question is "Aren't you ashamed of yourself?" It doesn't require an answer, since the question indicates that they think you ought to be. Parents and teachers ask that question when you've done something thoughtless, sinful, or simply stupid (or at least they think it was).

Why are we ashamed? I think it may be that we have lost confidence. We're afraid that others have lost confidence in us too. If we are ashamed of others, it is usually because they have disappointed us and caused us to believe a little less in them. Being ashamed is an awful feeling. We lack confidence in things, persons, and actions that cause us shame.

The apostle Paul is *not ashamed* of the gospel. He has confidence in Jesus Christ. He knows Jesus has the power to change a person's life. He had seen that power demonstrated in a thousand lives (including his own). I want to have that kind of confidence in the gospel. I want to believe Jesus Christ can make a difference in my world. I want to have such a confidence in Christ that I am not afraid to believe, not afraid to trust, not afraid to act with nothing to hide.

I'm ashamed of myself when I say things that hurt others. I'm ashamed of my friends when they do things they know they shouldn't do. I'm ashamed of a job that doesn't represent my best efforts. In each case my confidence is shaken. But "I am *not ashamed* of the gospel, because it is the power of God for the salvation of everyone who believes."

Lord, I am not ashamed of You. I want to see my world changed by the power of Christ. Help me to believe and act with confidence.

2

Amazing Grace

It is by grace you have been saved (Eph. 2:5, 8).

I suppose I have heard or sung "Amazing Grace" thousands of times. I've heard it sung in fancy churches by song evangelists (a little impressive), on the popular radio stations by people who didn't know what they were singing about (enjoyable but not very meaningful), and by a group of teenagers at camp (they sang it to the tune of "Gilligan's Island"; I didn't much care for it).

My friend Erin sang "Amazing Grace" in church one Sunday night. It is my most memorable experience of that song. She has a nice voice, but that wasn't the reason I remember it. She can follow the notes, but the musical skill wasn't the most memorable feature. In fact, she sang the song quite simply, without any kind of fancy vocal gymnastics. It was an ordinary, simple rendition of a familiar hymn. Yet, it was extraordinarily significant.

Erin had just experienced the grace she was singing about. She was very nervous before she sang because she didn't know the words and tune very well. She hadn't sung the song so many times that she took the meaning for granted. Amazing grace was a living experience for her.

She wasn't your typical high school student, just looking for a good time. Erin wanted to make her life count for an important cause. She just hadn't found that cause yet. She started coming to church with a friend and was intrigued by the "cause" of Christian faith. It was hard, however, for Erin to accept the idea that being a Christian was not something you achieved or earned. Finally, she accepted the idea of God's grace, His unearned favor for her, and believed in Jesus Christ for her salvation.

When Erin sang "Amazing Grace," she wasn't singing familiar words to a familiar song. It was a new song. It was her life story.

God, thank You for Your amazing grace that I experience in Jesus. I am not ashamed of that experience. Help me to share Your gospel with others so that they can sing the song too.

Junkyard Snow

We were therefore buried with him through baptism into death in order that, just as Christ was raised from the dead through the glory of the Father, we too may live a new life (Rom. 6:4).

I love a good snowfall. Last winter as I was traveling to Colorado to go skiing with family and friends, a light snow began to fall. The further we drove into the flatlands of western Kansas, the heavier the snow became. Where there had been a variety of colors and contours of the countryside, there was now a smooth blanket of white. Everything looked beautiful with the seemingly endless velvet covering of fresh-fallen snow.

Along the highway, a small junkyard littered with old, wrecked cars and trucks caught my attention. The yard looked like a fantasyland sparkling in the sunlight of a cold, crisp winter day. Everything looked so new, clean, full of life that I forgot it was a junkyard. I forgot it was full of abandoned wrecks, of little value to anyone. The covering of snow made me forget what was really there. I even commented to those in the car how beautiful that junkyard looked.

We drove on to our destination. After a few days of relaxing and skiing in the Rockies, we started back home along the same highway. The weather had warmed up, and most of the snow had melted. I vividly remember looking for that same junkyard to see if that magical scene still existed. I shouldn't have been surprised when I discovered that the junkyard was still just that, a lot full of discarded, rusty, junk cars. The snow had just covered the junk for a while. It hadn't changed the junk at all.

Sometimes we think God can help us by just covering up the junk in our lives so that everything will look nice and clean on the outside. The problem is that the junk is still junk. Nothing has really changed. When the covering wears away, the old junk is still there. Thankfully, that's not the way God operates.

When we become Christians, Christ's blood doesn't just cover up the junk in our lives; He offers us a new life, not a recycled or refurbished one. The old stuff is gone, and a new creation is born. We aren't the same old persons we used to be. The gospel makes a permanent difference, not a temporary one that lasts only as long as a single snowfall.

Lord, I'm not ashamed of the gospel. I have seen how it has made me new. The junk in my life wasn't very beautiful, no matter how much I tried to dress it up. Thank You for new life. It does make a difference!

4

New Beginnings

Therefore, if anyone is in Christ, he is a new creation; the old has gone, the new has come! (2 Cor. 5:17).

C. S. Lewis is one of my favorite authors. I love his imagination and the unique way he says things that are profoundly true, in simple ways I can understand. His *Chronicles of Narnia* are a fantasy masterpiece for children and adults alike. I'll never get too old to read them.

In the first chronicle, *The Lion, the Witch, and the Wardrobe*, Lewis tells the story of four earth children who travel through a bedroom closet to an imaginary kingdom called Narnia. This faraway land is under the curse of death, brought on by the power of the great witch. The four children are befriended by a lovingly powerful lion named Aslan. As the story proceeds, one of the children is taken captive by the witch and is threatened with death. Aslan, the lion, offers himself in exchange for the child. He is mocked and killed upon the cold, stone table of death. The children mourn for the loss of their friend and the prospect of living under the witch's curse forever. The witch rejoices, for she thinks she has finally won the battle over Aslan and his forces of good.

As I read the story, the plot sounded very familiar. It sounded strangely like the story of Jesus giving His life as a sacrifice for me. I am the child, and Jesus is Aslan.

I wept as I read the last chapter of the book. As the children cry for their slain companion, Aslan begins to move. His lifeless, shriveled body is filled with living breath. His spattered blood no longer mats his tangled mane. He stands tall, strong, and very much alive. Aslan is alive! The curse is ended. The evil of the great witch is defeated. Out of death comes life! That's good news.

That is the great news of the gospel. Jesus died for me. Jesus is alive for me. I am no longer under the curse of sin. I have life, not only because Jesus died, but because Jesus lives. He gave me a brand-new beginning.

Lord, You are the God of new beginnings. You make it Your business to bring that which is dead to life. I don't need to be ashamed about a message that is so powerful. I know a lot of spiritually dead people who could use Your message. Help me share it with them.

Learning to Love Again

I tell you the truth, whoever hears my word and believes him who sent me has eternal life and will not be condemned; he has crossed over from death to life (John 5:24).

I have had my heart broken a couple of times. That old popular song "Breakin' Up Is Hard to Do" is absolutely right. I remember each girl that I ever went out with (there weren't really that many). I also remember each girl that I fell in love with (not every girl I dated!). Breaking up with a couple of them was a heart-wrenching experience.

I remember one disappointment in particular. I fell in love during my sophomore year of college. She was blonde, cute, with personality. I thought she was the perfect girl to marry, so I asked her. She said yes and I was thrilled. Everything was going to work out perfectly. I was going to have a perfect wife, a perfect home, perfect children—a perfect life.

My fiancée and I were engaged for a couple of years. It seemed as if everything was going just as I had hoped. Then one day our relationship started to cool. You might know the feeling if you've ever broken up with someone. She called me on the phone and said we needed to talk. I expected what was about to happen, but I hoped it wouldn't. It did. She said she didn't love me anymore, and we should stop seeing each other. I begged her to reconsider. Perhaps she could learn to love me again. I could change something about me that would rekindle her love. It was futile. We broke up, and a part of me died that day—or so I thought.

Many months later I was going out with another woman (something I promised myself I wouldn't do, since I never wanted to get hurt that badly again). Before long a love was reborn in my heart that has lasted for the past 18 years. That woman became my wife. Out of a heart that I thought was forever broken came a new beginning of love.

That's exactly what the gospel does in our spiritual lives. It takes things that are dead and brings them back to life. Just as God's power raised Jesus from the dead, so God's power takes hope that has died in despair and brings new hope to life. He takes dreams that have faded due to life's circumstances and gives new ones, greater than the old. He gives dreams that are centered in His good will. The gospel is the message of new hope.

Thank You, God, for the new hope and love You give us in life. I'm not ashamed of the gospel that can bring such hope to others. I know people who need hope and love. Help me share Jesus with them.

A Plan Beyond the Dream

"For I know the plans I have for you," declares the Lord, "plans to prosper you and not to harm you, plans to give you hope and a future" (Jer. 29:11).

I hate feeling inadequate. You know the feeling? Having a job for which you're responsible and not having the skills to do it. Wanting to be on the basketball team, but not being quite good enough to make it. It's an awful feeling.

In junior and senior high school I was in the whiz math class. We were a small group of students who were always one year ahead of our grade in math. While everyone else was taking Algebra I, we were in Algebra II, and so on.

Since I thought I was good in math, I selected a career in computer science as my goal. I enrolled in a math-based track my freshman year of college and was automatically placed in the sophomore course on differential equations. I handled the first semester well. Then came the second semester of absolute failure. I never did catch on to what I was supposed to do. I couldn't solve a single equation on the final exam. I failed the test miserably! The awful reality set in that night as I lay on the bed in my dorm room. I wasn't good enough to fulfill the dreams I had for my life.

It wasn't too many weeks following my failure that God began to speak to me about what He wanted to do in my life. His plan for me had more to do with people than the Pythagorean theorem, more to do with preaching than programming, more to do with ministry than microchips. He was calling me to something beyond anything I had ever imagined.

God was calling me to another new beginning. In the midst of my feelings of inadequacy and failure, I heard God inviting me to a brand-new start at something that has been more significant and enjoyable than I had ever hoped for. Out of a broken dream, God brought new purpose and meaning. I don't know why I should be surprised at such a thing. God's plans are always beyond ours.

Lord, I am not ashamed of a gospel that calls me to live beyond my dreams, to live in obedience to Your plan for my life. I'm glad that Your plans are now my plans too.

It's Always Morning

Because of the Lord's great love we are not consumed, for his compassions never fail. They are new every morning; great is your faithfulness (Lam. 3:22-23).

My high school senior English teacher had a thing with sunrises. She would get up before dawn each morning to watch the sun emerge over the desert horizon of west Texas. In class she would describe the rich colors and exciting drama of those magical moments. On certain days, her eyes would fill with tears as she recounted the beauty of the morning light. She was trying to instill in us that same sense of awe.

Personally, I thought she was nuts! Why would anybody want to get up that early just to see the sun come up? If God really wanted everyone to see it, He would have programmed it for later in the day (say ten o'clock).

There is something about the sunrise, however, that I have learned to appreciate. It marks the beginning of a new day. I always have the feeling of being able to start over with renewed energy, a new perspective, and a sense of opportunity. I am a little less tired than yesterday. Yesterday's problems don't seem quite as difficult. Yesterday's doubt isn't quite as desperate. It's morning! It's a new day! The sunrise is a trumpet that blasts the arrival of a new day.

A wise, spiritual man once said that it is always morning for the Christian. I think I know what he meant. Being a Christian is being able to start over again, to have new hope in discouragement. To be Christian is to be new over and over again—renewed day by day by day. The power of the gospel is at work in our lives every day. Christ has the power to renew our hearts, soul, mind, and strength. It is true. It is always morning for the Christian.

Just as my English teacher watched the sunrise every morning, I want to experience a spiritual sunrise in my own life every day.

Father, thank You for loving me every day. Thank You for the spiritual sunrises I experience when I take time to let Your Word renew me. I am not ashamed of a gospel like that.

It's Not Just a Name

The disciples were called Christians first at Antioch (Acts 11:26).

What do you think about when you consider the names of the groups to which we belong? I'm always curious about the names that are given to the different groups on a junior high or high school campus. Some of the names, like jocks or cheerleader-types, have been around for a long time. Other names come and go with the cultural fads they represent. Skaters, bladers, druggies, freaks, nerds, punkers, brains, preppies, hicks, and several others that may be around would qualify in this group.

These names, or labels, describe people who belong in these different groups. I know that it is possible to stereotype people by placing them in the wrong group simply because they dress or talk a certain way. But more often than not people will dress, talk, and act in a way that identifies them with a particular group. Though we may dislike labels, they are usually accurate.

I was a jock in high school. I wore my letterman's jacket to school most of the time. I had to have the right kind of shoes, jeans, and shirt to match all the other jocks. We had our own vocabulary, our own corner of the lunchroom, and our own places to hang out on Friday night after a game. When you said "jock" at Stephen F. Austin High School, we knew you were talking about us.

I wonder how people perceive us when they know that we are called by the name "Christian"? I wonder if they describe us in a way that would be pleasing to God? Do you think they use words like *caring, honest, compassionate, trustworthy?* The first people called Christians weren't called that because of the way they dressed or where they hung out. They were called Christians because they identified with Christ. They lived as He lived. Though the name was first intended as an insult to that group of believers in Antioch, it became known as a badge of honor. It is a privilege to be called by Christ's name. It certainly is more than just a name.

Jesus, I am not ashamed to be called by Your name. When others know that I belong to You, help them not to wonder what You're like. May they see You in me.

People Not like Me

If you have any encouragement from being united with Christ, if any comfort from his love, if any fellowship with the Spirit, if any tenderness and compassion, then make my joy complete by being likeminded, having the same love, being one in spirit and purpose (Phil. 2:1-2).

When I go searching for friends, I often start looking for people who are just like me. The problem with starting with those kind of people is that there are just so few of them in the world. It really limits the field of potential friends to my brother, my mother, and one poor guy in the desert of central Nevada. I have come to the conclusion that there just aren't that many people in the world who share my concerns, have the same hobbies, enjoy the same sports, like the same foods, have the same taste in clothes, and so on. The world is made up of people who are not like me.

The great thing about the gospel is that it doesn't call us to like everyone else. It enables us to live in harmony and peace with people who are different than we are, but who are called by the same Spirit. That's the difference between uniformity and unity. The gospel doesn't call us to be the same, it calls us to be one—one in spirit and purpose, in Christ.

I remember attending a retreat recently with some of my friends. On Saturday afternoon we decided to hike along a trail for some exercise. As I watched the rest of the group head out on the trail, I noticed our distinct diversity. There were some rich, some poor, some really educated, some who hadn't gone beyond high school, some white-collar, some blue-collar, some neatly dressed, some not-so-neatly dressed. It was a ragtag bunch for sure. Yet, we all belonged to the same fellowship of Christians. We were brothers in Christ. That experience demonstrated for me the power of the gospel to create unity with people who are not like me.

Lord, thank You for a gospel that breaks down barriers between people. Help me to be a barrier breaker with people who are not like me. I won't be ashamed to do that!

A New World Order

It is for freedom that Christ has set us free (Gal. 5:1).

I would hate to work at Rand McNally and Company these days. You've probably seen one of their books. They make maps. The organization of the countries around the world has changed so drastically over the past couple of years that it is almost impossible to have an accurate atlas. Just about the time they have all the countries straight and correctly named, a major political breakthrough occurs and changes everything.

In recent months the Berlin Wall has been destroyed, and Germany, a nation that has been divided since 1945, has been reunited into one of the most powerful countries in Europe. More recently than the toppling of the wall, a major revolution in the Soviet Union failed and brought about the independence of many of the former republics of that socialist state. Europe and western Asia will never be the same again. The Middle East situation appears to be on the verge of some sort of negotiated peace talks. In some parts of the world, our enemies are now our friends, and some who were our friends are now our enemies.

The face of the world is changing. People are crying out for freedom. Churches are being renewed in areas where the public worship of God was forbidden. Bibles, which at one point were being smuggled through an underground network, are being publicly distributed in the city squares of Russia and Eastern Europe.

I often wonder what's going on. I think I know. *The gospel is making a difference in the world.* People are responding to the call of God to seek the abundant life provided in Christ. I believe that the gospel is not just somewhere in all this change, it is at the heart of it all!

My prayer for the world is that those who are seeking freedom, regardless of what kind of political system they may be ruled by, will find that freedom in Christ. It's the only kind of freedom that will really last.

Lord, You promised freedom for those who believe in You. May the gospel make people all over the world free today. Help us not to be ashamed of the gospel. No, in fact, help us to be bold to share the gospel with others.

I Didn't Go!

*Let us not give up meeting together, as some are in the habit of doing,
but let us encourage one another—and all the more as you see the
Day approaching* (Heb. 10:25).

I attended a large Christian conference recently and had the responsibility of listening to some of the participants evaluate the various activities that made up the schedule for each day. Most of the people responded in similar ways. They enjoyed everything and offered a few suggestions about how the conference might be improved next year. The answers were pretty standard.

One evaluation really interested me. It was different from the rest. The responder had some very negative things to say about the event in general. "Boring" and "Overrated" were a couple of the terms that got my attention. I wondered what had happened at the conference to give him such a contrasting opinion to those that I had been hearing. I decided to find out how much of the conference the person had attended. When I asked about the main sessions, he replied, "I didn't go to those." When I asked about some of the special workshops that were held, he replied, "Oh, I didn't go to those either." In fact, he had attended very few of the events associated with the conference. I wondered how he was able to make critical judgments about activities he didn't attend?

We sometimes make assessments about regular church services, youth group meetings, camps, revivals, etc., that are less than complimentary. The first question we must ask ourselves is, "Have I attended often enough to find out what really goes on?" Labeling something as boring or overrated simply because we don't *think* we would like it really isn't giving the activity a fair shake. I have a feeling that if we'll go often enough to really understand what happens when people who love Jesus get together, we'll begin to see that meeting together as Christians is one of the most helpful and "nonboring" things we can do.

Lord, I'm not ashamed of Your people. I want to be there when they get together to worship, study, and have a good time. Help me not to be one of those people who make a habit of not meeting together.

Clique Connectors

If it is possible, as far as it depends on you, live at peace with everyone (Rom. 12:18).

Say the word *clique* out loud three times. It has a kind of negative sound, doesn't it? Makes you want to stick your nose in the air in a snooty sort of way. It doesn't quite roll off the tongue with the spiritual rhythm of "love," "unity," "fellowship."

To be honest, I think cliques have taken a bum rap. I like cliques. I belong to several. If you think about it long enough, you probably do too.

Cliques are small groups of people who share a common identity or interest. Cliques are common. People like to be around other people who enjoy the same things. I hate watching a football game on television with someone who hates football. It's a miserable experience. Cliques are a natural way in which people organize themselves.

What makes cliques a problem at church or school is that they can become *exclusive*. They have the potential for leaving people outside the circle of friendship if those people don't have the same interests. Do you understand what I mean? People sometimes get left out of groups because they are different. They don't get invited to activities because they don't quite fit in.

Well, the dilemma of cliques is pretty clear, isn't it? They're natural, but they have tremendous potential to be destructive. How is the dilemma solved? What is needed are some *clique connectors*, people who are willing to open the doors of relationship from one person to another, to offer to be the link from one group to another. The gospel calls us to work through the natural separations (like certain interests) that come between people and become connectors, people who will live at peace with everybody.

We need not get rid of cliques, those groups of close friendships. What we need are not clique busters, but clique connectors. I want to live out the gospel by drawing people together with my love and friendship, rather than driving people apart with my own selfish interests.

Lord, the gospel of which we are not ashamed calls us to a rather large challenge—to live at peace with everyone. I want to be a clique connector in the friendship groups of my life. Help me to see the people on the outside and to draw them in by Your love.

What Can I Learn from You?

A man who lacks judgment derides his neighbor, but a man of understanding holds his tongue (Prov. 11:12).

I have been on more than a few mission projects in my life. I've participated in ministry trips in foreign countries, on Indian reservations, in the central core of major metropolitan areas, in a rural community, and in my own neighborhood. Each one has provided special memories. There's chickenhead soup in Guatemala, unbearable heat and humidity in Mexico, the porn district of Boston, hanging from the edge of a rooftop in Kansas City, the beautiful smiles of the Navajo children of Arizona—and a thousand more.

On the early trips I was always eager to get going so that I could build, fix, teach, preach, or save something or someone. I was God's special laborer, and I had a job to do. After all, isn't that why we go on these kinds of excursions? It always feels so good to give yourself away. In fact, most of the time spent in preparation to go was directed toward building, fixing, teaching, saving, etc., etc., etc.

The more trips I went on, the more clearly I understood that one of the major results of participating in a ministry project was what I *received* from the people to whom I was going to minister. You see, I got all geared up to give away but forgot about learning anything from the people where I was going.

What I'm talking about is a very subtle form of pride. I thought I was the only one who had something to teach. I forgot that the people in Guatemala, Mexico, Boston, Kansas City, and Twin Wells had something to teach me as well.

I must confess that on each trip I received much more than I gave. I learned the meaning of contentment, sacrifice, commitment, joy, and acceptance from persons that were living out the gospel much more genuinely than I was.

Now I've learned to ask *two* important questions when I prepare to go on a ministry trip. The first is "What can I do for you?" The second is "What can I learn from you?"

Lord, the gospel is not my private property. I'm not the only one who knows it or shares it. Help me learn from others who may be materially poorer than I, but who are spiritually richer.

God's Here

And surely I am with you always, to the very end of the age (Matt. 28:20).

Have you ever been in one of those uncomfortable situations where you wish you could vanish from sight? When I was in school, being called into the principal's office, even for something good, was never a cherished experience. Meeting your least-favorite teacher anywhere other than school, sitting with your parents at your high school's football game, or meeting the wanna-be love of your life without fixing yourself up might qualify as uncomfortable moments for you.

It might seem strange to you, but one of my most uncomfortable moments is one that happens often. I've had opportunity over the past 20 years to speak to a variety of audiences ranging from youth groups on retreats to adult camp meetings. I suppose that I have talked, taught, or preached over 500 times to groups that I didn't know personally. Something happens every time I go to speak. Just before it's time for me to begin, I get an uncomfortable feeling in my stomach. I usually say to myself (soft enough so that no one else can hear, obviously), "Ed, why did you say you'd do this? You're not really a good enough speaker to be standing up in front of all these people."

I confess to you, I get scared every time. But I have learned an important truth that helps. I've begun to remind myself that God's there too! That's the wonder of His Holy Spirit's presence in our lives. Wherever we are, He is there too! I'm not standing up in front of those strangers alone. God, through His Spirit, is standing with me. I don't have to think up a brand-new, highly creative message every time I speak. I just need to faithfully proclaim God's message—the gospel.

Now don't make the mistake of thinking that just because God's there, the uncomfortable things become comfortable. No, I still get scared. I still get that feeling in my stomach. But I won't give up. I won't give in to that fear. I won't stop telling others about the gospel. And you don't have to let that uncomfortable feeling stop you from doing the things that God is calling you to do. We don't have to as long as "God's there"!

Lord, the challenge to share the Good News with others seems so large. In fact, it makes us uncomfortable, even afraid, at times to think about sharing it. Help us remember that You're there with us, and by remembering, to overcome our discomfort and fear.

Goin' Through the Motions

By their fruit you will recognize them (Matt. 7:20).

I went to a high school football game last night. I was excited about going. I didn't know any of the players. None of the band members are in my Sunday School class. My children aren't cheerleaders. In fact, my daughter who attends the high school wasn't there. I went because I love high school football. The emotion of the team running through the paper poster, the rousing school fight song, and the simplicity of teenagers playing a game for fun rather than money makes an evening of football a real treat.

I noticed something, however, about the game last night that really troubled me. As I entered the stadium, I saw a large section of students standing in their seats. I thought they were really involved in the game. But as I got closer, I saw that none of them were even watching the game. They were too busy talking to each other to pay attention to what was happening on the field. I turned around once to see if they had noticed an exceptionally fine play. All I saw was the backside of 200 students. I don't know why they came to the game. Surely there are more comfortable places to visit.

The cheerleaders weren't much different. They spent more time looking at each other than watching the players. They missed a fumble recovery and a touchdown while they were performing for the people in the stands (who weren't watching anyway). I got the distinct impression they were cheering for themselves rather than for the team. I finally decided that the students and cheerleaders didn't need the football team to have a football game. They were just goin' through the motions.

To be authentically Christian—to live out the gospel—we must never just go through the motions. We can't just passively show up at religious events (church, for example) and expect something spiritual to result in our lives. Real fruit is produced by those who will take the time to plant, water, and tend the fruit trees. We can't afford to spend our Christian lives goin' through the motions.

God, I know what it's like to go through the motions spiritually. Forgive me for the times I've done that. I'll be more diligent about spreading, watering, and tending the seeds of the gospel in my life.

Mall Rats

He who has the Son has life; he who does not have the Son of God does not have life (1 John 5:12).

On any given Friday or Saturday night you can go to the local shopping mall in my community and find an enormous number of teenagers wandering up and down the mall. Some are there with their families. Others are there with friends, looking for something in particular to buy. Most, however, are at the mall just "looking for something to do." Many of them come to the mall every weekend with no particular purpose in mind. This group has a name. They're the mall rats.

It all sounds so innocent, but I'm kind of saddened by the fact that there are so many teens in my city who don't have much purpose in life beyond going to the mall. There's a huge world of relationships, places, experiences, truths, beauties, joys, and opportunities waiting to be discovered. Most of these things can't be found (or bought) at a shopping mall.

Jesus said that He came so that people might have life as God intended for it to be, with maximum fulfillment. My heart hurts for the mall rats of the world who are missing out on so much that life has to offer in Christ.

What are you doing next Friday night? I hope you have more purpose in life than just going out "looking for something to do" because you're bored. If you find yourself at the mall and you happen to spot a mall rat, offer a prayer of thanks to God that He has given you a great purpose in life. Offer a prayer for the mall rat that God's grace would be known in that teen's life. And if the opportunity arises, why not offer a word of hope and encouragement about the purpose you're living for. If enough of us will accept that challenge, we may be able to solve the mall rat problem.

Lord, thank You for the abundant life I have in Christ. I have purpose because of You. Help me to live that purpose every day, even on Friday nights.

Singing God's Song

In the same way, count yourselves dead to sin but alive to God in Christ Jesus (Rom. 6:11).

One of my favorite stories from Greek mythology is the story about Ulysses and Orpheus and their plans to overcome the hauntingly tempting music from an island that, had they been lured there, would have meant the capture of their ships and ultimately the defeat and ending of their journeys. Ulysses asked his men to tie him securely to the mast of his ship, blindfold him, and place rags in his ears so that he couldn't hear the tempting melody being played from the island. Ulysses had very little confidence in his ability to withstand the temptation.

Orpheus, a skilled musician and poet, chose a different method to overcome the power of the island's melody. He relied on his ability to sing and play a more beautiful song. As his ship passed, he played his harp and sang the most beautiful song he knew. He had a strong confidence in the fact that his music was more powerful than the music of the island.

Each of us is tempted in many ways by many things. We don't have much control over that. But we can control our reactions to each temptation. We can, like Ulysses, cowardly try everything within our own power to be strong, all the while thinking that we're just about to give in. Or we can choose to act as Orpheus did. We can have confidence in the power of the gospel to help us live as winners over sin. Since we have said yes to Jesus, we can have the power to say no to temptation. After all, we've died to sin, and we're alive to God in Jesus Christ. Greater is He that is in us than he that is in the world (see 1 John 4:4, KJV).

The best defense in most situations is a good offense. Instead of fearfully tying ourselves to a spiritual mast and stuffing rags in our ears so that we won't have to hear anything, let's start singing the beautiful song of the gospel of Jesus Christ and allow its melody to drown out the disharmony of the world.

Lord, I have confidence in Your song. When the "tunes" of this world start to capture my attention, help me to sing Your song loud and strong.

My Dad Can Beat Up Your Dad

Instead, whoever wants to become great among you must be your servant (Mark 10:43).

Remember those arguments you used to get into when you were a kid? They often started something like this: "My bike is better than your bike." That would usually elicit a response like, "Oh yeah? Well, my dog is smarter than your dog." Such a statement would lead to an all-out comparison of every personal possession, teacher, friend, brother, sister, pet, home, family car, neighborhood, even favorite television hero. The argument would proceed down this endless road until the final comparison that settled everything, "My dad can beat up your dad," was made. For some strange reason that seemed to end the argument. I must admit that I never once saw two dads meet in the park to fight it out to see whose dad really could win the battle.

These arguments were all about power. Whoever had better, bigger, tougher, or more had the power. That kind of power is used to dominate others. The arguments between adults, groups, nations, and superpowers are basically the same as the childish comparisons of fatherly wrestling skills. They're just a little more sophisticated.

Jesus talked a lot about power. He said that power was something you used to help (serve) others. When we use power as God intends, we don't dominate. We share power with others.

I have power. You have power. Everyone has some sort of power. It may be the power of knowledge, or influence, or popularity, or money, or age, or belonging to the right crowd, or social status, or anything that gives you an advantage over others. We have a choice about how we'll use it.

Jesus' disciples argued about how they were going to use the power Jesus gave them. They wanted to be great. Jesus said the road to greatness went by way of the Cross, where they had to first give themselves away. Our road to greatness (true power) makes the same stop.

Jesus, You had such incredible power while You were here on earth, yet You chose to use it for others rather than for yourself. I want to use the power You've given me in the same way. Help me to empower others today.

Anything but a Missionary

Then I heard the voice of the Lord saying, "Whom shall I send? And who will go for us?" (Isa. 6:8).

We call the youth leadership council at our church the "senate." To qualify for a position on the senate, a teen must commit to being an example of faith, consistent in attendance at the youth group activities, and dependable in carrying out responsibilities.

We don't elect people to the senate, since that can easily turn into a popularity contest. Individuals fill out an application giving the reasons they'd like to be on the council, committing to the expectations, and writing out a brief testimony of their faith.

I can remember when my daughter, Kimberly, wanted to try for the senate. She was in junior high, and most of the other applicants were high school age. She filled out the application one Sunday afternoon and brought it to me to read. She wanted me to make sure she'd written everything correctly before she handed it to the youth pastor.

I was thrilled she had taken the initiative. I reviewed her application with pride. I had to smile when I came to the last section in which she wrote out her testimony. It read something like this:

I became a Christian when I was a child. I love the Lord with all my heart, and I'll do anything He wants me to do (except be a missionary!).

Kimberly was being honest. She really did love the Lord *and* really didn't want to be a missionary. I asked her why she'd made that exception, and she muttered something about jungles, bugs, and strange-looking food. The only problem with Kim's honest commitment is that it wasn't quite accurate. To love God with "all my heart" means that she won't make exceptions about what He can do with her life.

A lifetime commitment of complete obedience to God's will is necessary to be genuinely Christian. We can't afford to make a list of exceptions where God's will is concerned. Do you have one of those lists?

Kim has since changed her testimony and wiped out the exception. She still isn't anxious to become a missionary, but she is willing. Are you willing to do whatever God asks?

Lord, thank You for reminding me that to love You with my whole heart is to commit my whole life to You. I want the best for my life, and Your will is best. Make me willing.

The Hot Seat

Do not let any unwholesome talk come out of your mouths, but only what is helpful for building others up according to their needs (Eph. 4:29).

Have you ever noticed how much easier it is to say a put-down than it is to offer a word of encouragement? It's just more natural, I guess, to humorously cut people down than it is to say something affirming that will build them up. I think I know why that is. Saying nice things and giving encouragement makes us look so . . . so . . . well, I guess I'll just go ahead and say it—so nice and Christian.

My wife, Nancy, teaches sixth grade. Every once in a while she'll have her class participate in something she calls the hot seat. One person is selected from the group to sit in a chair in the middle of the circle. Each student is asked to say one nice thing about that person. No put-downs are allowed. The compliments and affirmations range from the superficial (I like your sneakers) to the very significant (I can trust you with a secret). Hot seat is a great activity. You may want to suggest it sometime for your class, youth group, or family.

I have some questions about hot seat, however. Why do we have to plan a special activity to say things that are positive? Why don't we just say affirming things to each other naturally? Isn't that the way those of us who are Christians are supposed to talk to each other anyway?

The apostle Paul knew that the more natural way of talking is to say things that are unwholesome, things that keep us and others from becoming whole. That's why he said that people who have been changed by the gospel are people who speak differently from that. We are challenged by God's Word to say only those things that build others up according to their needs.

The next time you're tempted to say one of those cute put-downs to a friend, acquaintance, or family member, why not catch yourself and put that person on your hot seat and say a kind word instead.

Lord, it is so easy to talk to and about others in such negative ways. I want my conversation to be different from that. I want to build people up, not tear them down. With Your help, I'll do it today.

I Forgive You

Lord, how many times shall I forgive my brother when he sins against me? Up to seven times? (Matt. 18:21).

I never did like breaking up fights. I often had to do it as a parent, Sunday School teacher, referee, counselor, etc. Oh, I'm not talking about fistfights or wrestling matches. I'm talking about the verbal fights we all get into from time to time where we spar with words. These kinds of fights usually start over some insignificant matter and end up resembling World War III. You've probably been in a couple in your life.

When the battle calms down enough to figure out just what happened, apologies and forgiveness are usually in order from both directions. When I am bigger than the people who are fighting, I usually command the combatants to say, "I'm sorry" and "I forgive you." When the combatants are bigger than I am, I usually ask them politely to say the words. While everyone's emotions are pretty tense, the two people will usually respond through clenched teeth with a mumbled voice, "I'm sorry," or "OK, I'll forgive you." God knows they don't mean it, I know they don't mean it, they know they don't mean it, everyone on God's earth knows they don't mean it!

Then I usually get upset and harshly order, "Say it again, and this time as if you mean it!" But, the apology or the forgiveness never comes out quite right. There is no sincerity in it. You'd think I'd learn after all these years that repentance and forgiveness are things you can't force people to do. They have to want to do it.

Being Christian means that we are repenting and forgiving people. We want to do those kinds of things because God has forgiven us. Peter's question, "How many times shall I forgive?" was really a question of ought and should. Jesus answered Peter's question by telling a story that reminds us that we should want to forgive every time, since God has forgiven us.

"I forgive you" are hard words to say to someone who has hurt us. But isn't that exactly what God has said to us in Christ, even though we have hurt Him deeply with our sin? When God says, "I forgive you," we hear the sweetest words that can be spoken.

Lord, I am a forgiven person today. I want to be a forgiving person as well. I want to do it, not because I have to, but because I desire to, as a result of what You've done for me.

Anything but Discipline

So then, just as you received Christ Jesus as Lord, continue to live in him, rooted and built up in him, strengthened in the faith as you were taught, and overflowing with thankfulness (Col. 2:6).

I'll admit it without any apology. I don't like discipline. I'd rather eat than exercise. I'd rather play than work. I'd rather sleep late than get up early. I'd much rather watch a football game on TV than go out and work in the yard. Postponing things until tomorrow isn't that hard for me to do. Let's face it, self-discipline is not one of my strong points. I'd almost rather do anything than something that requires more discipline. Maybe you can identify with me.

I have, however, gained a gem of wisdom over these last 40 years of living. Most of the things in my life that are really worth having or doing require hard work and discipline.

I spent over half of my life as a student at various levels. The longer I was in school, the more I realized that I needed some self-discipline to survive. Those overnight term papers just didn't cut it in graduate school.

I have a wonderful wife (18 years of wedded bliss). It's fun being a husband, friend, and lover. But my marriage takes work and discipline to make it all God designed for it to be.

I've been a Christian for as long as I can remember. I enjoy being a Christian. I enjoy going to church. I enjoy the fellowship of my Christian friends. But to be a true disciple (there's discipline even in that word) of Jesus Christ means that I must commit myself to the disciplines of the Christian life: reading the Bible, prayer, worship, and service. These are the avenues by which my faith is strengthened and I become "rooted and grounded" in Him (Eph. 3:17, KJV). Now that I think about it, maybe I don't mind the discipline at all. The benefits are phenomenal.

Lord, You know how undisciplined I can become at times. I want to be rooted and grounded in You. Help me make Your spiritual disciplines a part of my everyday life as I live in You.

God's Plumb Line

Your word is a lamp to my feet and a light for my path (Ps. 119:105).

I never was much of a builder. I've built a few things in my lifetime, but nothing real fancy—a clubhouse in the third grade, a tree house in the fourth, a footstool for my first apartment, and patio covers for a couple of houses. These were OK, but each one had some flaws. In my haste to get these things built, I didn't take the time to use the principle of the plumb line to set everything straight *before* I started putting all the pieces together.

The plumb line is one of the oldest tools used to judge whether a wall, building, or post is straight up and down. The principle is simple. Because of the consistent law of gravity, a string with a weight tied at its end, when hung from a nail at the top of a post, will always be straight. You can judge the straightness of a wall by comparing it to the string.

What happens, then, if a wall is crooked or warped? The solution is to make the wall and the plumb line match. But you can't fix the wall by bending the plumb line. No, the only way to make the wall straight is to fix it to match the straightness of the line.

The Bible works like a plumb line. Sometimes we have a hard time judging if our lives are reflecting God's love and glory as much as we want them to. We need a standard that is straight so that we can compare our lives. The Bible can be that *plumb line.*

God has given us His Word as a *lamp to our feet and a light for our path.* If we want to see how *straight* our lives are, we need to check them against God's Plumb Line, the Bible. If we're a little warped, the Plumb Line will help us change. That's what the gospel does best.

Father, thank You for Your Word. In a world that is so dark and gives so many options about which way to go, it's great to be going in a definite direction for the journey and with a lighted path on which to walk.

Common Sense or God's Sense

Do not conform any longer to the pattern of this world, but be transformed by the renewing of your mind (Rom. 12:2).

Webster's Dictionary defines common sense as practical judgment or ordinary good sense. I knew that before I looked it up. Common sense is the kind of sense everybody is supposed to have. It's the kind of understanding that a person ought to have to be able to figure things out naturally. It's very practical. Common sense is supposed to keep you out of danger, trouble, and sickness. Here's a list of well-known common sense phrases:

Wash your hands before you eat. (It's healthy.)

Don't pick a fight with people that are bigger than you. (It's stupid.)

Save something for a rainy day. (It's smart.)

Don't pick your nose in public. (It's just plain gross.)

People I have talked to recently say that the thing they like about Christianity is that it's so practical. The Christian faith makes good common sense. Living the Christian life works out better than living on the wild side. Or so they say.

I am beginning to understand that becoming a Christian and living genuinely as a Christian may be one of the most impractical things you can do. It seems a lot more practical to me to love my friends and hate my enemies. But Jesus said that I need to love them both. How impractical! It seems a lot more practical to me that if I want to get ahead in life, I need to figure out a way to be in charge as the leader. But Jesus said that I need to be a servant if I want to get ahead. How impractical! Common sense tells me that if I want to save my life, I'd better protect it carefully. But Jesus said that if I want to save my life, I have to be willing to lose it. Talk about impractical!

God's sense isn't all that common. It calls us to some pretty radical thoughts and actions. That's part of the transformation that takes place when we allow our minds to be renewed (reoriented) by the power of the gospel—a gospel, by the way, which is the most uncommon message one could ever hear.

Father, You have called us by an uncommon message to an uncommon life. Help us to live beyond our own common sense and accept Your sense as our guide for living.

Banquet or Potluck

Come, let us bow down in worship, let us kneel before the Lord our Maker (Ps. 95:6).

Do you know the difference between a banquet and a potluck? Of course you do. The main difference is what you have to bring to each. People don't bring anything to a banquet except an appetite (and perhaps some money!). If people brought only their appetites to a potluck, everyone would go hungry. At a banquet people come into a large room, sit at fancy tables, and wait to be served. At a potluck, the group works together to set up the tables, set out the food, and clean up the mess when it's over. There's a huge difference between a banquet and potluck.

Do you know the difference between banquet worship and potluck worship? Maybe not. I figured out the other day that I have been to 7,397 worship services since I was born. That's a lot of church for someone as young as I am.

When I was younger, I tried every trick in the book to keep from getting bored in service. I counted holes in the ceiling tiles. I played word games like putting a phrase like "underneath the back porch" after each title in the hymnal. I became an expert at solitaire, ticktacktoe, and dot-to-dot.

I tried all those things because I thought worship was like a banquet. I thought I could come and sit and wait to be served my weekly dose of music, Scripture, announcements, and sermon. If I didn't like the "menu," I could leave and complain about how boring everything had been simply because it didn't please my taste.

I failed to understand that worship is more like a potluck. I am responsible to bring part of the "meal" to worship. Just like any good potluck, I also am responsible to share my contribution with everyone else by singing, praying, following the Scripture reading, and listening carefully to the sermon.

So what about your worship? Is it a banquet or a potluck? I'm convinced it should be more like a potluck. I've always liked potlucks more anyway. I seem to get more out of them.

I know that worship is important to You, Lord. Your Word speaks so often about it. Help me to worship You with more of myself. I really do want to worship well.

A Big Hole in the Ground

*In the beginning God created the heavens and the earth. . . . God saw
all that he had made, and it was very good* (Gen. 1:1, 31).

The Grand Canyon is one of my favorite places in the world. The vast
expanse of rock and sand formations cutting into the mountains of north-
ern Arizona is one of the most magnificent natural wonders I have seen.
The word *awesome* gets overworked at times, but the Grand Canyon is
one of those genuinely *awesome* sights.

I have visited the canyon several times. Once I had the privilege of
hiking to the bottom (hiking back out wasn't quite the same privilege).
Each time I go I am reminded of the majesty of God. The Grand Canyon
bears His signature. The magnificent creation has all the marks of the
magnificent Creator.

On one visit, I was seated on the edge of the canyon with my feet
dangling over. The brilliant orange sun was setting in the western sky, and
the canyon's colors came alive with shades of red, orange, purple, and
blue. As I sat there in the quietness, people emerged from a nearby forest
and came upon this incredible sight. Their conversation turned from loud
voices in trivial discussion to soft whispers of wonder at the beauty of the
sunset. They were confronted with the signature of God. The canyon rim
became a sanctuary.

Soon after this event, I was talking to a friend who had never been to
the Grand Canyon. I encouraged him to go and see one of God's great
wonders. I was shocked by his response. He shrugged his shoulders and
replied, "There's nothing that great about it. It's just a big hole in the
ground." Just a big hole in the ground? He's got to be kidding! Obviously
he's never seen it.

I am afraid we often miss God's glorious signature. In the midst of all
our manufactured glitz, we have become dulled to the wonders of creation. In the process, we run the risk of becoming dulled to the Creator.
May God's beauty never become a "hole in the ground" for you. If it does,
you've missed a glimpse of God.

*Lord, how full of wonder is Your creation. Help me to see Your signature in
my world. May seeing it help me understand You better and serve You more
faithfully.*

Saturday **27**

They Kept Praying

Devote yourselves to prayer, being watchful and thankful (Col. 4:2).

Across the street from the school where I teach is a large building that looks like a huge chapel with an attached dormitory. The building used to be a cloistered convent. The order of nuns who lived there were the Sisters of Perpetual Adoration. Their practice was to make sure that at every hour of the day or night there was at least one member praying in the chapel—perpetual prayer. When the order first began, there was an abundance of nuns to share the task. But after years of round-the-clock praying, the number of sisters began to decrease to the point where only a few were left to do all the praying. But they kept on praying.

When their leaders decided there weren't enough nuns to justify such a large building, they ordered that the Sisters of Perpetual Adoration be moved to another convent. But in the meantime, they kept on praying.

The appointed day for moving finally arrived, and the sisters packed their belongings in a truck and prepared to leave. But during the packing, one of the sisters was still in the chapel. She just kept on praying.

When the last box was packed and all the doors had been checked, a few men prepared a small kneeling bench in the back of a pickup truck. As the group prepared to leave, the men went to the chapel and picked up the sister who was still on her knees and placed her at the kneeling bench in the truck. All the while she kept on praying!

God hasn't called most of us to be Sisters of Perpetual Prayer (I couldn't qualify even if I wanted to). But God has called all of His children to be devoted to prayer. Prayer allows us an opportunity for praise and thanksgiving even when we're not at church. Prayer allows us to voice our concerns to a God who hears, understands, and acts on our behalf. Prayer allows us the privilege of showing our love and care for others by talking to God about them. Let's join the sisters and keep on praying.

Father, I probably don't talk with You as often as I should. I'd like to make conversation with You a daily event. Help me build the discipline of prayer into my life.

Authentically Christian

Since we live by the Spirit, let us keep in step with the Spirit (Gal. 5:25).

Going to the meat department at the supermarket has become a challenge in recent years. The challenge lies in trying to locate all the different items that are made from turkey. There's turkey ham, turkey hot dogs, turkey pork chops, turkey bratwurst, turkey Polish sausage, turkey hamburger, turkey sausage links, and the ever-popular turkey bologna. I am beginning to wonder if there is some form of meat that can't be made from turkey.

All of these various foods have one thing in common. They are imitations of the real thing. They may look like genuine ham, pork chops, hamburger, or sausage. They may even taste like the originals. But when you come down to it, they're imitations made from turkey.

There are a lot of Christian imitations around. These imitations may try to look like Christian faith by dressing up in the right clothes and going to the right places. They may even sound like true Christian faith by using the right vocabulary and singing the right songs. But these substitutes are still imitations unless the essential ingredient is authentic.

We set out on a pursuit 28 days ago to find what it means to be authentically Christian. I think we may have found our answer in the essential ingredient of Christian faith. To be Christian means to be transformed by the power of the gospel of Christ Jesus. To be Christian means to belong to a community of faith (as small as your youth group or as large as all Christians everywhere) that tells the story of the gospel by its word and its example. To be Christian is to live a life that bears witness to the character and discipline the gospel enables us to have. To be Christian is to live and walk by the Spirit of God in a lifelong journey of faith.

The essential ingredient of authentic Christian faith is the power of the gospel at work in us. I am not ashamed of a gospel like that!

"Grace and peace to you."